Th… …le of Ea…ter

Bethan James and Paula Doherty

Everyone came out to cheer and wave when Jesus went with His friends to Jerusalem. They loved Jesus and the stories He told about how much God loved them. Jesus had also healed people who were ill. The blind could see. The deaf could hear. People could walk again.

'Hooray for Jesus!' they shouted. 'Jesus is our King!'

They waved palm branches and they spread their cloaks on the ground for the donkey to walk on.

But not everyone was happy. The religious leaders were enemies of Jesus, plotting against Him.

It was nearly time for the Passover feast. Jesus and His friends met in an upstairs room to have supper together.

But first, Jesus took a towel and a bowl of water and began to wash the hot, dusty feet of all His friends.

Peter tried to stop Him – surely Jesus was His master, not His servant! But Jesus wanted to teach His friends to take care of each other.

'Love one another as I have loved you,' said Jesus. 'Then everyone will know you are my friends.'

When they sat down to eat supper together, Jesus was thoughtful. He shared some bread with His friends.

'This is my body, broken for you,' He said. Then Jesus shared with them a cup of red wine. 'This is my blood, shed for you.'

Judas Iscariot left the room. He went to tell Jesus' enemies where they could arrest Him – for 30 silver coins.

That night, Jesus went with His friends to a garden of olive trees. He asked His friends to watch and pray with Him. Then Jesus prayed to God, His father.

'Help me to do the right thing and be brave,' He asked God.

When Jesus went back to His friends, they were not keeping watch – they were tired and had fallen asleep. But now it was too late.

Judas was coming through the trees with a group of men armed with swords and clubs. They arrested Jesus and marched Him away.

Jesus was taken to His enemies, the religious leaders. They asked Him lots of questions, trying to find anything that would give them a reason to have Him killed. But Jesus hadn't done anything wrong – so they said it was a crime for Him to say that He was God's Son.

Meanwhile, Peter waited in the shadows outside.

'You're one of Jesus' friends, aren't you?' said a servant.

'No!' replied Peter.

'Yes, you were with Him!' said another.

'No, that's not true,' Peter lied.

'You even have the same accent,' said a third.

'I told you! I don't know this man,' said Peter.

Then Peter heard the rooster crow. It was morning, and Jesus was marched away to the Roman governor. Peter was so ashamed that he cried.

Pontius Pilate could see that Jesus was an innocent man. But he sent Jesus away to be beaten. The soldiers put a crown of thorns on the head of Jesus and made Him carry His cross to a hill outside Jerusalem.

There He was nailed to the cross. 'Father, forgive them!' Jesus cried out. 'They don't know what they are doing.'

Jesus died that day between two thieves, while His mother Mary wept for Him.

Jesus' friends were shocked and frightened. How could this happen?

Jesus was taken down from the cross by two friends. One was a man called Joseph from Aramathea. The other was Nicodemus. They wrapped Jesus' body in a linen cloth and buried Him in a rock tomb on a Friday night. A heavy stone door was rolled over the entrance.

Some of His other friends followed and saw where His body was laid. The women wept because their friend had suffered a cruel death.

Very early on Sunday morning, the women came back to the tomb bringing herbs and spices – but the stone door had been rolled away and the tomb was empty!

They saw two angels there.

'Why are you looking for the living among the dead?' they said.

At first the women didn't understand – but then Mary Magdalene heard Jesus speak her name! Then she saw Him. Jesus had died – but now He was alive!

Jesus came to see the disciples, who were hiding in a locked room. They were very pleased to see Him even though they could not understand what had happened.

But Thomas had not been there. 'Unless I see Jesus for myself, I cannot believe He is alive,' he told them later.

Then Jesus came again. He showed Thomas the wounds in His side where a soldier had put a sword, and the nail marks in His hands and feet.

Jesus explained that He had to die so people could be forgiven of their sins. But God had given Him new life – the new life God gives to everyone who trusts Him.

Later, seven of the disciples went fishing on Lake Galilee. They caught nothing all night.

At dawn, Jesus called to them from the shore. He showed them where to find a big catch of fish and they all had breakfast together by the lake.

The friends knew that Jesus had died, but now He would live forever. Jesus promised that when He returned to God in heaven, the Holy Spirit would come and be there to help them always. He wanted them to tell everyone the good news that they too could know God's love and forgiveness, and to show people God's love in the way they lived.

First edition 2018

Editorial Director: Annette Reynolds
Art Director: Gerald Rogers
Design and pre-production: Doug Hewitt

Printed in China

Published 2018 by CWR, Waverley Abbey House, Waverley Lane, Farnham, Surrey, GU9 8EP, UK.

Registered Charity No. 294387. Registered Limited Company No. 1990308.
For a list of National Distributors visit www.cwr.org.uk/distributors